# Overcoming the Diagnosis

by
Channing Ewell

Watersprings
PUBLISHING

Overcoming the Diagnosis
Published by Watersprings Publishing, a division of
Watersprings Media House, LLC.
P.O. BOX 1284
Olive Branch, MS 38654
www.waterspringsmedia.com
Contact publisher for bulk orders and permission requests.

Copyrights © 2020 by Channing Ewell

All rights reserved. No part of this publication may be reproduced, distributed, or transmitted in any form or by any means, including photocopying, recording, or other electronic or mechanical methods, without the prior written permission of the publisher, except in the case of brief quotations embodied in critical reviews and certain other noncommercial uses permitted by copyright law.

Printed in the United States of America.

Library of Congress Control Number: 2020902614

ISBN-13: 978-1-948877-26-8

# Table of Contents

Introduction .................................................................... 1

Chapter 1: Back to the Beginning ............................... 3
   Trace Your Oppositions ............................................. 3
   Face the Opposition ................................................... 4

Chapter 2: Unfamiliar Territory ..................................... 7
   God Causes Change When We Don't Want It ............ 7
   God Wants You Uncomfortable ................................. 8

Chapter 3: The Change ................................................ 11
   Your Seasons In Life Will Change ............................ 11
   You Can't Stay Where You Are ................................ 12

Chapter 4: Training Ground ........................................ 15
   You Must Equip and Prepare Yourself .................... 15
   Condition for the Position ........................................ 16

Chapter 5: Time tor Battle .......................................... 20
   You Will Have Battlefields ....................................... 20
   Fight and Be Confident In Who You Are ................ 21

Chapter 6: The Scars of Battle (Returning Home) ...... 24
   Your Wounds Will Heal ........................................... 24
   What's the Prescription for Your Affliction? .......... 25

*Chapter 7: The Diagnosis* ............................................................ 28
    You Must Make Adjustments .................................................. 28
    Prepare For the Fight of Your Life ........................................ 29
    Never Lose Your Momentum ................................................... 31

*Chapter 8: Going Through the Process to Overcome* ............ 34
    You Must See It From God's View ........................................... 34
    We Must Do the Natural Before The Supernatural ............. 35
    Have Patience And Be Open-minded To The Changes ........ 36

*Chapter 9: Erasing the Issue By Medicine or Miracle* ........... 40
    You Can Depend On God ......................................................... 40
    Don't Look Back, Look Forward and Step Out On Faith ..... 41

*Chapter 10: The Victory – Overcoming the Diagnosis* .......... 44
    Living Your Life With No Limit ............................................... 44
    Smile And Know That You Are A Winner ............................. 46

*Chapter 11: The New Journey* ..................................................... 49
    Go and Pull Others Out Of The Darkness Into the Light .... 49
    Don't Put a Label On Your Diagnosis .................................... 50

# THANK YOU

I want to take the time to first and foremost thank God for having pre-eminence and lordship over my life. For giving me the wisdom, strength and memory to write this book and share this testimony with all who will read it.

I want to thank my lovely queen, brown sugar, friend, partner, my rock, and my wife, Laquita A. Ewell. You have been a driving force and have been there for me through all of the challenges, loving me and praying me through it all. I thank the Lord for you, and for your help to convey my thoughts and ideas in this book. Thanks for giving me the title for this book.

To my children Malachi and Nadia, my other gifts from God, thanks for loving me and being such awesome children.

Thank you to the late Apostle Nathaniel Holcomb and Pastor Valerie Holcomb of the Cathedral of Central Texas Christian House of Prayer (CHOP) for feeding me the word of God and changing my life. For impacting my life and causing me to mature, grow and get closer to God.

I want to send a special thank you to Elder Tyrone Holcomb for giving wisdom, guidance, and direction on writing this book and mentoring me throughout the process.

Iron sharpens iron and I'm grateful to these men of God who have been such awesome brothers and spiritual fathers to me. Tim Britt, Brandon Baggett, Dr. Gregory Cruell, Julian Hartley, Bishop Clarence Williams, Elder Holloway, Jesse Gainey and many others who have sown so much wisdom and word into my life.

Thank you, Ms. Kimberly Wallace-Zamarripa for allowing God to prophetically speak through you to me about writing this book. You are a mighty vessel of God and bless you for your obedience. Many blessings to you and your family. I pray for increase.

I dedicate this book to my godparents Mark and Angelita Howell for showing me what strength through adversity looks like in the loss of your son. I thank you for giving me permission to use his name in my book. I love you guys beyond words. Chris rest in heaven sir and thank you for pouring into me and my family.

I also dedicate this book to all of my fellow veterans who suffer from life's challenges. Know that you are not alone in what you are going through, and you can overcome the diagnosis, living your life without limits.

# Introduction

In life we go through trials and valleys that change our lives. What do you do when the doctor has life changing news that will impact your way of living? What if they diagnosed you with issues like Post Traumatic Stress Disorder (PTSD), Dementia, or even some type of cancer? Some of us would start to worry, stress, or say my life is over, I'm dead. We depend on the doctor for the medicine, the chemotherapy and all types of treatments for our issues. What If I told you that there is a cure to all of these issues?

Everyday there are veterans that commit suicide from bad news. However, life doesn't have to end. I've gone through many storms and have touched death myself, so I can sympathize. There is only one Doctor you need to depend on, and He is better than man's medicine. This Doctor has the prescription for every single pain, affliction, disease, and issue that anyone faces. Well ladies and gentlemen, I have found that Man, that Doctor, His name is Jesus. I would like to share a story of a young man who has been healed of issues like PTSD, MTBI, Migraines, knee pain, shoulder pain, body alignment issues and many other things that I will talk about in this book. It is because of God he is still here, and he can say as a person, Christian, husband, father, brother, and veteran that he is an overcomer and you can be one too.

So, let's take a journey through the life of Christopher H. Wallace and how he overcame life's challenges: physically, mentally and spiritually. He had faced many issues, from drug addiction, suicide attempts, family issues, depression, mental illness, PTSD, and many other things but overcame them all. If he can do it, you can do it too. So I challenge you to trust, believe, and have faith in God for your healing. Whether God does it by medicine or miracle He can and will heal you.

# CHAPTER 1
# Back to the Beginning

*Trace Your Oppositions*

Christopher was born in Gainesville, Florida, but spent most of his life as a military brat. He had a lot of challenges throughout his life. His mother left him and his two sisters, when he was about 5 or 6 years old. His mother spent time out in the streets on drugs and dealing with other issues. At the time, he couldn't comprehend why she left him at such a young age. Christopher had to endure a lot of verbal abuse from his father growing up and couldn't understand his father's actions. However, God knew the path He had set for him.

There was a lot of built up anger toward his dad because of his mom leaving. He was a momma's boy, so you can understand why. He went through school frustrated and upset about his life, getting into fights at times and making terrible decisions. He became rebellious as a teen and was in trouble at school, a lot of times getting suspended for fighting, stealing, and smoking. At age 16, he was put out the house over a disagreement with his father. The oldest sister had just moved back in and he got blamed for something he didn't do. So, he decided to stand up for himself and got put out the house. He spent a few nights on a cold park bench up the street, he even stayed with some friends from school from time to time. After about a week or two in the streets, Christopher called the Deacon and Deaconess from church, who later became his adoptive parents. They took him in and showed him that there was a better way.

We have to trace where we started and look at the cause in order to face the opposition along the way. Chris was angry with his dad, but God used his adoptive parents to break through the barriers. He had a black heart like Pharaoh. Pharaoh refused to let the Children of Israel go and it took God slaying his first-born son to change his heart. Chris had so much built up aggression against his father, only an act of God would change him. He just wanted a normal life, but God had other plans. He had to face the demons and not run from them, because eventually they always catch up with you. If David could face the giant Goliath, why not us? We spend so much time trying to figure how we can do it, or how we can beat the system, but God has always had the master plan. It's not up to us to figure out what only God can work out.

## Face the Opposition

Eventually Chris got his first job working at the Courtyard Hotel. It was given to him by a brother from the church. It was there that he came across his greatest opposition. He was driving around without a license and staying with a friend. One day he accidentally bumped into another car while at the movie theater and got arrested. It was a night that God would make an invitation for him to make a decision. He sat in jail for 6 hours, and that is all it took for him to see he needed to make a change. He had to leave South Carolina, or he was going to be in more trouble than if he stayed. So, he asked a friend to take him to see his adoptive parents one last time before he got on the Greyhound Bus bound for Avon Park, Florida to his uncle's house. They cried and prayed for him and told him this was the best decision he could make. Chris felt uncomfortable, but he knew this was what God wanted for him. To take him into unfamiliar territory to get a fresh start. So, he moved to Florida. It was time to face a new place and new people in unfamiliar territory.

Christopher's adoptive parents changed his perspective on life and his image. He thanks God for them and their children, they embraced him as a little brother. For some reason he had always been in and out of church seeing people pray and talk about God, but he never understood God like he does now. He loved the drums at church and being in the choir. He also enjoyed going to cut lawns with his adoptive family. I, myself, had cut so many yards when I was younger, I lost count. He gained so much knowledge and wisdom on life. To this day, he believes that moving to Florida was the fresh start he needed, and that it helped him put things into perspective.

Are there events in your life that have turned you dark, cold or unforgiving? Are there adversities or oppositions that have caused you to retreat and wallow in your misery? Are their places in your life where you look back and say "Oh my God, I'm glad it's over" but you can appreciate the journey it took to get there? Let's take a moment and pray that you are released and that you are able to face, trace, and erase the past hurt, pain, and feelings of inadequacy.

Channing Ewell

## *Prayer*

*Father in the name of Jesus. We pray against the opposition and adversities in our lives. We thank You for the journey that You choose for us, and I thank you for allowing me to trace and face my issues in this world. God, You have taken me through this valley and now into unfamiliar territory. You have shown me that it is better to be uncomfortable, than comfortable with You and life. You have shown me not to be settled where I am. Abba, in the name of Jesus, continue to show us what to trace and face. Please erase that which we don't need in our life.. God let Your will be done and not ours. It's in Your Son Jesus' name that I ask.*

*Amen*

**Scripture References:**
Deuteronomy 32:5, 1 Timothy 6:20, Psalms 61:3, Exodus 23:22

# CHAPTER 2
# Unfamiliar Territory

*God Causes Change When We Don't Want It*

Chris left South Carolina late on a Friday night, he had so much built up anger inside for his father at the time. He traveled alone on a greyhound bus with two big duffle bags, a backpack, a CD player, drawing book, and $100 cash. As he stared out the window Chris thought about where his life was going. Chris knew that it was a change that he didn't want, but it had to be done. He didn't want to leave but he knew he had to before he self-destructed. God had a plan for his life and was writing a story that was beginning to unfold. Chris didn't know at the time that he was sailing on a ship that God was the captain of, and he was charting for unfamiliar territory.

Sometimes in life, things can be going the way we want it to and God will cause a shift. Not every midcourse correction in our life is wanted, but it can be necessary. Everything works out for your good, but not necessarily when you think the time is good. God may make a major shift and you're left wondering about what is really going on. Although every change may not be wanted, it is always necessary if God is doing it.

Channing Ewell

*God Wants You Uncomfortable*

So, Chris arrived in Avon Park, Florida safely and his Aunt was there to pick him up. They talked all the way to the house and she said to him "this is a fresh start." He took it for what it was, and she also invited him to church. Chris had a lot of family in the area that all looked after him. On Monday after he settled in, his uncle took him to school. Chris sat down with a guidance counselor and she told him there was no way that he would be able to graduate unless he made all A's and high B's. She told Chris it would be impossible in her opinion, but he looked at her and said, "I got it." Then thought to himself, "I will make her a believer." Chris unknowingly had just set himself up by speaking life into his situation.

Filled up with so much anger Chris needed to find a way to let it go. He pretty much kept to himself at school. Football season had already started, so he decided to join the band. He was in band at his other school playing in the percussion section. Chris played the snare and trap drums. He also played in the New Generation Gospel Choir at school, headed by Mr. Washington, one of the teachers there. It was here Chris sat under a lot of different drummers, Alfred Golden, Chad Washington, and Travis Anderson. These guys all had their style and they used to pick on Chris at times for being the new kid on the block. Chris took everything they played and showed him, and learned to develop his own sound and style of playing.

He still had a void in his life and to fill it, he joined track. Chris ran the 400, 4X4, 400 hurdles and 800. Chris's coach said he ran like he had a demon in him because he ran so fast. He was always running from something, and the irritation on his face showed his anger. Chris found out that instead of fighting and getting into trouble, that going to church and playing drums was a great avenue of escape. He played drums at Vision Christian Community Church. He played a lot of traditional contemporary music along with gospel music. This was new for Chris. He saw the positivity of it all and he also got a job as a cashier and stock person at Big Lots. Chris was doing good and becoming comfortable in his new environment.

He became uncomfortable again when the state test came out, the FCAT (Florida Comprehensive Assessment Test), which he needed to pass to graduate. It was hard, especially the math section. He was stressing it so much, he thought it was impossible to pass. He buckled down, took a FCAT prep class the high school was offering and studied his butt off. He passed it the first time and he was proud of himself. Chris had a meeting with his guidance counselor and she was in tears because she said he did the impossible, he was going to graduate. He was excited, but he thanked God because God did it, not him. Chris had all A's and one B, and was proud.

Chris had learned that being comfortable with God was never a good thing, because you can become so carnal. When we become uncomfortable with Him then God can move and shape us into what He wants and needs us to be. Chris had to be uncomfortable and have pressure on him in order to excel. He had to trust, believe, and apply the Word while doing the work. God wants you to be uncomfortable so that He can apply pressure to stretch you and challenge you just like He did to Chris. In the end you will see the result of victory.

Channing Ewell

## *Prayer*

*God, I thank You for the change. For allowing me to be uncomfortable and not comfortable with You. I thank You for the change even when I didn't want it. I am grateful for how You have ordered my steps and how You guide me through the valleys and the issues of life. Father, You have always been there for me even when I could not trace You or understand Your plan for my life. God, Your plan is perfect even when I do not understand it. Lord, help me to trust You more and believe in You even for the inside change. I ask all of this in Your Son Jesus' name,*

*Amen*

**Scripture References:**
Jeremiah 50:34, 1 Samuel 14:25, Genesis 43:1, 1 Kings 9:18, Psalm 91, Haggai 1:1-15, Haggai 1:23, Leviticus 27:33, Genesis 45:22, Job 17:12

## CHAPTER 3
# The Change

*Your Seasons in Life Will Change*

High school graduation was here, and Chris was excited but still felt empty inside. His father was coming down with his sisters and his mother. He still felt that something in his life was missing. This season was a season of challenges and victory for him.

Graduation night Chris walked the stage when his name was called, with his family cheering he raised his hands like he had won the boxing title. It felt good for him to receive his diploma. Afterward he walked up to his older sister and gave her a hug and smiled and looked her in the eye and said, "You can do the same thing. Go back and get your diploma." They had never always agreed on things as they had to grow up early in life, especially her. After their mother left them she had to step into those shoes. She had some other issues going on as well and their little sister was just an infant when their mother left. His older sister has fought many battles; she dropped out of high school in her senior year with one class to go. She was pregnant at the time with his nephew, Michael, she never went back to finish that one class. He said this to his older sister at graduation because Chris knew what was in her, she is intelligent and full of life. She has always been someone that he looked up to. She has been like a hero at times and other times a thorn in his side, but he still loved her.

Today, she is doing so much better then at that time, and he is proud of her. She has been locked up, out on the street and more. Chris can say that she is an overcomer. Today, she has her GED, is taking college classes, raised three beautiful kids; two of which are high school graduates. Her son is currently serving in the United States Army and her oldest daughter graduated high school early at 16, she is aspiring to be a fashion designer; with her youngest, a sports star, starting high school very shortly. So you see, seasons change in our lives and things come up, but it doesn't mean we need to quit. That ladies and gentlemen, is victory and a huge accomplishment. So even when your season changes keep going and looking forward, even in the storm. Just remember that God is the one who is orchestrating and guiding you through that season.

## You Can't Stay Where You Are

After graduation Chris was still working at Big Lots and at the church, but he was feeling empty. He had a couple of colleges that were interested in him for track, but Chris didn't want to go to school anymore, or really run the 400m. He also had the Army scouting him, and the recruiter came to a lot of his track meets. Chris didn't want to stay in Avon Park because he felt in his heart that his season was up, God moved him there to finish high school with minimum distractions and trouble. He knew he couldn't stay there because he would have got caught up in the streets. He also wanted to get away from family as well.

Chris called his recruiter and told him, "I am ready for a change, a different environment." Chris was used to the military because his father was a retired Air Force veteran and a lot of his family served as well. He joined at a time of war and conflict, but this was the path God choose for him, not college. To be honest, he would not have been focused in college, so God knew exactly where he needed to be. Chris still had a lot of built up anger for his father and needed to go somewhere where he could get it out of his system. Chris needed to grow more, that is why we can't stay where we are in life, and with God.

You must also understand that seasons change in your life, but God will never change. We will become content and comfortable with where we are, and we will never grow without pressure and being uncomfortable. Joining the military to him is where the real journey and growth started. God set him up and put him on a quest for greatness.

Remember this, if you stay where you are even when the diagnosis is given for your situation, you won't grow, things won't change, and you will eventually die. You have to be hungry for the cure to your personal issues and you may have to move to another place to get it. We are to hunt and chase God for the cure in our life, never be settled or content for where you are. Don't make where you are your final resting place. Your final resting place is with God. Until He decides to call your name and bring you home, keep moving and searching for Him. Your life is like a game of chess, it is built on strategy and a case of patience and wisdom. A chess game may not be won in one day. There are chess matches that go on for years because one move that you make could set you back or forward. Eventually you

Channing Ewell

have to make a forward move on the board, in the chess match you can't stay where you are on the board forever. My question to you is, what's your next move? Are you going to stay where you are and let the dust settle and be content?

## *Prayer*

*Father, we thank You for what You are doing in our life. We thank You for the seasons and how You change them to show us who You are. I thank You for Your grace and Your mercy to be patient with us even when we get it wrong. I thank You for allowing us to be uncomfortable and under pressure. I thank You Father for putting this fire in our heart to not be settled where we are, but to keep us moving and growing to another place in You. In the name of Jesus, show us the next move to make in our life to move forward, give us wisdom to change with the seasons and adapt to the season we find ourselves in. God, I thank you for remaining the same in every season. Guide us Father to where we need to be and let us see You in the season. Let us get the diagnosis for our issue and press forward for the cure, which is You. We ask this in the name of Your Son Jesus Christ, Amen*

**Scripture References:**
Genesis 45:22, Malachi 3:6; Hebrews 7:12, Leviticus 27:10, Proverbs 24:21, Galatians 4:20, Job 14:14

## CHAPTER 4
# Training Ground

*You Must Equip And Prepare Yourself*

When joining the military Chris found himself in Fort Sill, Oklahoma for Basic Training. He still had an attitude and anger built up in him, so he thought he was unbreakable to his Drill Sergeant's. He learned quick that he wasn't prepared for what they wanted him to become, and that is a soldier. He eventually met his match with Drill Sergent Stevens who took a special interest in him. He used to do a lot of pushups because of his attitude and one day he got broke down after class for not answering back.

After that, he changed, he stopped trying to be angry and mad with his leaders and started learning and obeying them and executing training. He became a physical trainer, squared away soldier, and leader. It all happened on the training grounds of Fort Sill, Oklahoma and Fort Bliss, Texas. In the military there are different training grounds depending on your task and your job.

Before you go to your duty station you must first be equipped to be a soldier and prepared to execute whatever orders are given to you by your leaders and superiors. It is like that with

God, we must be tried and proven, equipped and prepared to go out to help others. We also have to be equipped and prepared for the diagnosis, ready to move and execute. For this, we need a training ground to train on and be equipped with the means to learn what God needs. You need a church home to be trained at. Now, being equipped and prepared is not an easy task. While on the training ground you will make mistakes, but you must learn from them.

Forget about what you think you know and open your mind and ears to hear the instructions. You must also condition yourself mentally and physically as well for life's challenges and tasks. When you receive the diagnosis, you must equip and prepare yourself mentally and physically. That could mean going through counseling, chemotherapy, or other medical treatments. Whatever you have to do in the natural until God heals you, prepare yourself and be equipped to overcome and go through so that you can help someone else go through.

## Condition For The Position

When being conditioned for a position it can mean many things, physical, mental, spiritual, or medical. There are many things that conditioning requires. Whatever you have to face, whether it's death, emotional crisis, diagnosis of cancer, other medical issues, divorce, marriage, losing a job, promotion, speaking engagements, make sure you're prepared and conditioned. Conditioning can involve many things, when Chris would get ready for his Army Physical Fitness Test (APFT). He would run three to four miles the day prior, stay hydrated, prayed, prepared himself mentally, focused, and got a good night's

## Overcoming the Diagnosis

sleep. For a lot of us, conditioning for a medical diagnosis involves our mind. No one wants to get the bad news of Post-Traumatic Stress Disorder, Mild Traumatic Brain Injury, a loved one dying, having cancer, or a host of other issues. We want to shut down and ask God why me? Why not you? It is not for you, but your diagnosis is for others to help them go through and help them know they are not alone.

I here so many stories about veterans killing themselves because of PTSD. There are so many programs out there to help, I can testify and tell you that it is very curable. I suffered with it for years but today I can say that I am better and healed of it. I went through months of vigorous counseling sessions talking about my blast from Iraq, losing soldiers, experiencing closeness of death, and living life after a blast. Counseling was how I beat PTSD. You have to condition your mind, PTSD is a mind disease, and so is MTBI. I had doctors tell me my mind was gone, or I have short-term brain memory loss. I got the diagnosis and gave it to God; my memory is blessed, I still can play drums, learn music and hang out with my family. We make the diagnosis worse than what it is, and then we just give up when the diagnosis is given to us.

We have to stop worrying and have faith in God, faith starts when we stop worrying. Just because a doctor tells you that you have cancer doesn't mean that you will die. My little sister, had stage two breast cancer and today it is in remission. My cousin had breast cancer and today it is in remission. So, who's report will you believe? Their cancer is in remission because of their faith, now yes, they went through chemotherapy and the natural things but they never gave up hope. They conditioned their body and minds for the next phase until God did the supernatural. You have to go through and take that medicine and treatment until you see the manifestation of God.

God is very real, I have seen Him work in my life and my families lives. I am an overcomer of the different diagnosis' that doctors have given me. I am here today, writing this book, playing music, loving life and my family. Prepare, condition, and equip yourself with the tools you need. The root of every diagnosis is in your mind, that is where the enemy fights us all. If he can get your mind then he has you. Your mind is powerful and so is your tongue. Speak life to your situation and stay away from toxic thoughts and toxic people and relationships. Speak this over yourself, confess it and possess it! *"I am a winner, an overcomer, and I am equipped and conditioned for the position."*

## Prayer

*Father, we thank You for this time and we ask that You open our hearts and minds to be equipped and prepared for life's diagnosis and challenges. We ask that you condition our minds from any negative, and toxic thoughts. We are winners and overcomers in Your eyes. Father, we are champions and we walk in our healing and victory and are confident in this. We confess and possess it in the name of Jesus. We count it done and we claim it and thank You for this time and for Your Son Jesus. For allowing us to come to You with permission in this prayer. For the word says, "No man can come to the Father but through His Son Jesus" (John 14:6 KJV). We thank You and we love You. This is our prayer to You God in the name of Jesus we ask.*

*Amen*

**Scripture References:**

1 Corinthians 16:4, Ezekiel 46:10, Matthew 5:41, Isaiah 52:12, Zechariah 8:21, Genesis 11:7, John 6:44

## CHAPTER 5
# Time for Battle

*You Will Have Battlefields*

In life you will have a battlefield. For example, a boxer's battlefield is a boxing ring, a doctor's is a hospital, and the military can be a place like Iraq. Another major battlefield can once again be the mind. The hardest fight that a lot of us have to face on a daily basis, can be making simple decisions to deciding what you want to do with your life. Once you have trained it's time to go onto the battlefield. You have all of the tools and equipment that you need to go fight.

Chris had to prepare for Iraq and his very first, and only deployment. He could say that he was tough and ready to defend, but honestly, he was afraid and scared, not just about deploying but scared of leaving behind his wife and kids. His unit made a stop to go through some more training before they flew over to their final destination in Iraq. So, his unit was all settled in and a few months had passed. One day in June, his living quarters were hit by an IRAM, a powerful rocket. It was powerful enough to throw Chris from his bed and he landed head first on the ground. His roommate was worried that he had snapped his neck.

All Chris remembers is waking up in the middle of the blast and yelling to God to protect him and his unit. He expressed to God that he wasn't ready to go, that he had so much more to do. He remembers his roommate pulling toward him and throwing pillows on them and praying with him. If you call upon the Lord, He will answer you and be with you in trouble and honor you with long life, which is found in Psalms 91. Then a call of all clear was made and they had to go through accountability.

All the training kicked in, looking for people, putting out fires, and tending to the wounded and dead. Chris had a hard time seeing dead bodies, it is not something that you can just forget or ignore.

Sometimes you will have dead and wounded on your battlefield. In war there are always casualties. The battlefield is never pretty. If you are going through chemotherapy for cancer or other issues the battlefield can be hard and require endurance even when you're tired. For Chris, he had to go from one battlefield to the next one, from physical to mental. He had suffered a concussion, had swelling on his brain which caused headaches and migraines. He had to learn to fight and be self-confident and know that he was a champion and victorious overcomer. When going through your battlefield, make sure that you have all your equipment and are well-trained and equipped for it. Your battlefields can be anywhere, and anything, so don't always expect the field to be easy or fair.

## Fight And Be Confident In Who You Are

In your battlefield, fight and be confident, know that you have been given strategy to help maneuver around the enemy.

Sometimes you have to study your opponent and get into their mind because they are doing the same thing regarding you. Every enemy has a weakness, sometimes we are our own weakness and our mind is the main reason we fail and lose ground, or the battle. Being confident means being smart and showing that you are ready.

When we get the diagnosis, we get scared instead of being confident that we can and will beat the diagnosis. Know who you are and whose you are. Stop letting doubt and fear take over your mind and kill your confidence. Get in there and fight, who told you that you can't make it. Fight when you take those blows of life that may bring down your confidence and self-esteem, fight. Fight for your life and the cure to your life's battles. Level the playing field and put fear in the enemy, there are a lot of veterans that give up on life and don't want to deal with family, they would rather let anger and depression kill them off when they have so many programs and options out there if they just believe and go to the hospital. My fellow veterans, fight.

I know of a young woman named, Loren who has been fighting for years while paralyzed but still praising God through it. She never complains but fights on her battlefield with God as her General. I went to the hospital to pray over her. Seeing her gives me confidence and tells me that if she can go through, what's my excuse, why give up? She has had countless surgeries and treatments for her condition, and she is still here because she is confident in who she is and knows her worth.

Know your worth and fight for what you believe in. This young lady didn't allow the enemy to take her mind. I have even seen her mother come through life's challenges with her daughter and even she has learned to love God, after she had lost everything. You can win the fight, let your confidence be the weapon and allow it to strike the blow. Sometimes the practice of silence goes a long way, choose what you say and make it positive and not negative. Stay in the fight like Loren and claim victory in advance with confidence.

## Prayer

*God, I thank You for my battlefield and training and for equipping me for the battle. God, I ask You to keep my mind clear and positive and allow me to fight in confidence. I thank You God for Your strategies. Father, I press and fight the good fight of faith like David did against Goliath, I claim victory on my battlefield against the enemy and his devices in the name of Jesus I pray.*

*Amen*

**Scripture References:**
Matthew 27:8, Job 5:23, Exodus 9:25, Leviticus 25:34, Genesis 49:30, Isiah 5:8, Acts 1:19, Exodus 22:5, Judges 9:32, Psalm 91

# CHAPTER 6
# The Scars of Battle (Returning Home)

*Your Wounds Will Heal*

After the battle your wounds will heal but you will have scars. The blessing in the scars is that they tell a message for others of what you have gone through. They are to help others who need to heal or get through their battle and recover from their scars. To do this we must reveal those scars to others who may have similar scars, or people who need to see someone who has gone through a battle and came out victorious, maybe scared but not broken or destroyed by it.

When Chris returned from combat, he had scars that were not physical, but mental. He was struggling with headaches and migraines. But most of all his biggest battles were PTSD, Post Traumatic Stress Disorder and MTBI, Mild Traumatic Brain Injury which effected his memory. MTBI, is a brain injury that can cause issues like, Migraines, Dementia, Chronic Fatigue Syndrome, and many other complications. This was caused by the blast where he suffered a concussion that should have killed him because he landed head first, and from what

## Overcoming the Diagnosis

the doctor said it should have broken his neck. The blast came from an IRAM, Improvised Rocket-Assisted Munition. These are munitions that are made from large metal canisters and it is launched from a vehicle like a semi-truck. It is a flying IED, Improvised-explosive device, these devices are propelled by 107mm rockets from remote model sites. These IRAMS cause mass casualties and death. Chris was able to survive the blast but lost seven battle buddies, including two close soldiers in his S-3 shop. Your scars do not have to be physical, as you can see sometimes the most dangerous and hurtful scars are the ones that you don't see.

Many veterans deal with PTSD, the scar you don't see. They are irritable, angry, confused, and upset at life and the world. Especially after a situation like what Chris experienced. PTSD is not just from combat but can be caused in many environments: lawyers get PTSD, regular employees at work, those in construction or just being at Walmart. PTSD is very real, it can be treated and you can be healed from it. My question to you is, do you want the prescription for your affliction, or do you just want to blame the world and be mad at the world?

### What's the Prescription for Your Affliction?

Speaking of prescriptions, Chris had to use a lot of different medications struggling with migraines and anger issues. Coming home from the deployment a lot had changed at home with his family, dealing with agitation and also getting used to a non-combat zone was a challenge.

Going to church was the key to his healing and playing the drums was an avenue of escape. At first Chris didn't want to play the drums anymore because of the loud booms and noise. However, the Lord spoke to Chris one night and said your healing is in drums and music why do you fear drums? God had a plan to heal Chris and drums were part of it, along with counseling sessions from his pastors and therapy as well. It was part of the prescription for his affliction, so he was obedient and went back to playing the drums, pushing through the adversity and challenges. Sometimes inside our affliction we have to push and move forward to recovery like a woman giving birth to a child, or that bodybuilder getting that max on the bench press in his reps. Growing pains are a part of the push.

Your prescription may not be like how Chris's started, but we all have a prescription for our affliction. Whether it is medicine or miracle, God has something for our affliction, He has the perfect cure, but we have to push to see what that is. This Push comes with adjustments and changes to our lifestyle and how we used to do things and also before getting the prescription we must have a diagnosis. Before God can do the supernatural we must do the natural and see our doctors and get that diagnosis. From there, your journey begins. God is the Captain of your ship. It is the floor where you begin, not the ceiling for that is where the journey ends. So, in the next chapter we will explore the diagnosis and how to get beyond it.

## Prayer

*Father, I thank You for my scars and for allowing them to heal so that I can show others who need to see them to help them get through their situation in their battle. God in the name of Jesus I thank You for my afflictions and allowing me to go through my battle, Father I am grateful that You have the prescription and medicine for my affliction. You said that it is good that I was afflicted Psalms 119:71. So God I thank You for that. God, I thank You for peace and giving me strategy and insight for my afflictions. Keep my mind focused and my heart stayed upon You. We ask this in Your Son Jesus' name,*

*Amen*

**Scripture References:**

Psalm 119:71, 132:1, 106:44, 34:19, 119:153,

Job 5:6, 36:15, Genesis 1:18

## CHAPTER 7
# The Diagnosis

*You Must Make Adjustments*

Coming home from deployment you have to make adjustments that are not easy, especially when coming home to a family. For Chris it was a long struggle at first, getting used to the kids again and the loudness. He wouldn't even discipline his kids for almost six months due to fear of going overboard and possibly hurting them. Adjusting and having patience was key to his success after deployment. Moving to Fort Hood, the biggest military installation, was an adjustment for Chris but also a blessing to get out of Fort Riley where he was deployed from and getting fresh perspective on life. He got to his new unit and got settled in, about 3 months in he was having a rough day dealing with Land and Ammo Operations in the Battalion S-3 shop. He got into it with one of his superiors that got in his face while he was sitting down, but his Sergeant took care of the issue. Then his Sergeant sat down with Chris and asked, "What is going on?" He also asked, if he had been through counseling for PTSD.

Chris responded that he had a little at church and when he first got back from deployment once.

## Overcoming the Diagnosis

Sergeant said, "I need to send you to the program that Fort Hood has because you are no good to me unless you get help."

So, Chris went to see a counselor. At first, he wouldn't talk, but the counselor never gave up on him. Eventually, he started to open up in the individual and group session. One session he recalled the traumatic event from deployment and shared the positive side of it. He began to talk about how coming to Fort Hood was a great adjustment and how God really saved his life and changed him. Chris would never forget the tears his counselor cried when he told her. She shared that she was crying because of his faith and how powerful a testimony he has.

At the end of the day Chris was diagnosed with severe PTSD and MTBI. Chris went through about six months of counseling. He was in for the fight of his life. He had a long way to go with the doctors and family making the adjustments to become an overcomer. After the diagnosis is given, you must make the adjustments, some are hard, others may be easy. You must fight and keep the momentum going, never backing down even when the days get hard.

### Prepare For The Fight Of Your Life

Down this road to recovery Chris had to go through some pain and endure some issues. One of the biggest challenges is dealing with wanting to commit suicide several times. Chris had some days that were not easy. One time he wanted to blow out his brain. He was living in San Antonio working at the VA and he had some rough days. He came home that day and wanted to end it all. He had a gun and had it loaded. He sat on the edge of his bed with the gun in his hand. One of Chris's friends called just to check on him and see how he was doing, and he never pulled the trigger. It's amazing how God shows up on time, God truly stepped in and used a friend. Sometimes God will send help just when you need it, you can always depend on God to be with you in your storm. He will never leave you. He is always with you as He was with Chris.

Another fight that Chris went through is a drug addiction because of his migraine headaches. You would think I was talking about cocaine or marijuana, but your local prescription drugs are just as dangerous, if not worse. Chris went through numerous medications trying to gain control of the pain. This fight was intense. The doctors tried every medication they could think of, tests were done, and theories were made. He was prescribed a specific medication from the military called Tramadol which is a narcotic that is given for severe pain. He was taking so much of it that the addiction came. He started taking more than the prescribed dosage to the point he was like a zombie, zoning out even in church services while playing with the orchestra.

Chris was in another world popping Tramadol like it was candy. Tramadol is just as powerful as cocaine and doctors are starting to see it now. Eventually, when Chris moved to San Antonio, he went to the VA there and his doctor took him off all of the medications and started him on Botox injections. Chris took so many medications that it caused him to gain weight, be depressed and many other issues. He had a pharmacy at home because of all the medications. Today, he has a cabinet at home, to remind him of what God has done for him by taking him off the medications that he no longer uses. God had to, like a child getting off of breast feeding, wean him off the medications. It's not as easy, but it can be done. There are so many prescriptions given to people that have many side effects and can cause a dependency on those medications. They take the pain away for a moment, but it returns so we take more of it trying to numb that pain.

Again, God has the prescription for every affliction and pain we face, we need to be dependent on Him and not the medicine. The fight we face with all of this is in our mind. That was Chris's challenge, his mind, which is the hardest fight for so many veterans and people in general, if we lose are mind then everything goes with it. We must stay in the positive lane and not the negative one. Our mind is the most powerful weapon we have that God gave us. When the fight is in our mind we need to pray and think about our actions and be mindful of the distractions and our reactions because they have consequences. When you fight, you're going to take hits and develop scars and experience pain and fatigue.

*Never Lose Your Momentum*

When in a fight we will get tired and want to say I quit and give up. If Chris would have given up he could have killed himself, been a drug addict, or even been turned over to a reprobate mind. However, he didn't because he kept the momentum going. He pressed his way through to the end which resulted in his healing and living a better life for him and his family.

A boxer takes a blow but keeps going and punches back. For example, in Rocky II, we see Rocky fighting Apollo Creed in the end, and he is tired, hurt, bloody, bruised, and can barely stand up. In the end, Rocky hits Creed and they both fall down. Both are trying to get up and Creed is out of it because his body is tired, the referee is yelling and Rocky is on the ropes climbing in pain, he is tired, but he gets up to his feet just before the referee reaches 10 and wins the match. Rocky used what momentum he had left and didn't give up.

We fall down but we get up because we are all champions. Chris has beaten all of the odds in life from being put on the street to being blown up and living life beyond the blast. He kept his momentum going, he never gave up even when he could. Many people don't recover from addictions, but he did, that proves that it can be done, and it is possible if you believe. It's possible to be healed from PTSD. It's possible to recover from financial hardship. It's possible to have your marriage healed. It's possible for God to open multiple doors and hold them open for you to decide to step out on faith and walk through them. All things are possible to them that believe (Mark 9:23). Don't lose your drive in your storm your momentum is based upon what you put into it and it's up to you to keep it going or give up and let it die.

## Prayer

*God in the name of Jesus, we thank You for our storm and the diagnosis in our life. God forgive us for doubting and getting tired in the fight. Father keep us in the fight and help us make the necessary adjustments so that we can keep the momentum going and come out in victory. Father let us fight the fight of faith and believe that all things are possible with You. God shows us the next steps in our diagnosis and the path, so that our healing can take place. God when the diagnosis is given, we ask that you create the plan and path we need to follow, whether it is done by medicine or miracle in the name of Jesus we confess we are healed, healthy, blessed, and prosperous. We confess and possess our healing mentally and physically in the name of Jesus we pray.*

Amen

**Scripture References:**
Mark 9:23, 10:27, Matt 19:26, 13:11, Daniel 1:12,16, Ecclesiastes 9:11, Romans 12:2, Luke 24:45, Psalm 35:1, 1 Timothy 6:12, Exodus 14:14, Deuteronomy 3:22, 2 Tim 4:7

CHAPTER 8

# Going Through the Process to Overcome

*You Must See It From God's View*

When we go through our valleys and tribulations, we must see it from Gods view. God has a plan for all of us and we have to go through some things to get to the end result. What we go through and experience is not for us but, it is actually for others. You might be asking, "What do you mean for others?" What I am saying to you is that you are going to come across people that are going through some issues, troubles, storms, and valleys and because God has brought you through you will be able to show them how to get out. In 1 Corinthians 10:13, it talks about with every temptation God creates a way of escape. Sometimes that way of escape is you, you can help others not make the same mistakes you did or show them how you made it out of your storm. Your scars are for others not you, when God places people in your life with those situations it will be like a reflection of yourself, you will see yourself because you went through and came out.

Chris had to see his story from God's view. All of the

addictions, pain, adjustments, and the diagnoses was never intended for him but for you and others reading this book. At times, we never see the big picture we just see the struggle and wonder if we will make it out. We even say that God can heal us by miracle but sometimes that miracle is by going through with the doctors and getting treatment before God can do the healing. We always want the supernatural part of things but, we forget we have to go through the natural first. Chris had many challenges to face but through faith and believing that God could heal the things he went through he kept his momentum and drive to see the end result of all that he had faced.

## We Must Do the Natural Before the Supernatural

Chris had to do the natural thing by going through so many medications and seeing doctors, putting on weight, being depressed, wanting to commit suicide and other things. He not only had to deal with medical issues but family issues. He had to adjust at home and was also fighting for his father's love. In Chapter 1, you see the struggle of being put out the house and having to find himself. Chris had hated his dad for years but always loved him deep down. It's not good to have a black heart like Pharaoh did with the children of Israel, but there are people out there that do and Chris was one of them. Chris spent so much time trying to force his father's love that he started to hate and have anger toward him.

One experience he recalled was his wedding day. He was getting married and he called his father and he remembers his father hanging up the phone on him. That hurt him beyond what he could say but he got married and moved on from it. Chris just wanted his dad to be proud of him and be happy for him. He had to endure this fight for years but eventually he let go and let God have the issue, and with time and patience God healed. Today, he and his father have a better relationship. God healed it supernaturally, but Chris had to do his natural part by experiencing it and then making a decision to step out of the way and let God do it His way.

His big thing was that he wanted to break the curse because his father had issues with his dad and Chris wanted to break the cycle with his father so that it didn't pass on to his son. His healing came truly when his grandfather passed away, his relationship with his dad was restored. The blessing was his grandfather got it right with his dad before he left this place, so Chris got it right with his father. They sat down for a couple of hours and got things off their chest. After years of frustration and anger they apologized, forgave one another and that is the revelation of a difference and shows us that all things are possible with God. When we let go to let God then we can move on, when we do our natural part then God can do His part. Remember, faith without works is dead (James 2:26).

## Have Patience and Be Open-minded to the Changes

The thing that we all deal with in life is not having patience for things especially when in our storm. We keep questioning when is it going to end, or when is God going to do what He said? The answer is when we stop murmuring and complaining. Just be silent, have faith and patience in God, and be openminded to change during the process.

Chris had to deal with change because he thought he was going to do 20 years in the Army and retire, but God had other plans for him. The change was medically retiring at 12 years of service because of complications beyond his control. He had to be open-minded, it was a huge change for him and his family. He had to trust and believe in God and step out of his comfort zone of that military life. He had to transition to civilian life, which for a lot of veterans is not easy, but Chris made the transition and went on leave.

While job hunting he found himself moving from Killeen to San Antonio and doing security at Methodist Main Hospital. The blessing in this is that he got to be among so many people and be a light for people who were sick and going through. One of the nurses said he was different than most of the guards, he had patience and a loving spirit about him. Whenever he got called in for a situation, the way Chris handled it was with patience and being open-minded and a loving person. Eventually, Chris transitioned to the Department of Veterans Affairs in San Antonio as an Operator because the site of more death started to take its toll on him.

One night he came into work and had to work the children's Emergency Room. He came into a situation where a child had died from drowning in a pool and all of the family was there. It really messed him up because the doctor came to him and asked him to tell the family to leave after four hours. The medical examiner had to come pick up the body. Chris will never forget the sweetest little girl came up to him while he was observing the family during their grieving time in the hospital room, she asked him, "Is he sleep?"

Chris responded, "Yes sweetie, he is."

She replied back, "Can I go in?"

Chris said, "Check with you parents first."

She gave him a hug and said, "Thank you, you are nice."

After work he asked the doctor, "Why did you ask me to tell the family to leave when it's your job?"

He said, "Chris your delivery and your approach to people are awesome as well as your patience and love for others."

Chris didn't know people were watching him like that, but he understood why. He went home and cried because of seeing such a young child dead, he told his wife that he could have been one of their children. Chris had enough, God knows just how much you can bear. He saw that in such a short time at the hospital, he had touched lives and his job didn't want to let him go. They even tried to offer him a position in Dallas, but he turned it down.

Chris went on to the VA, and eventually transitioned out of that job to not working. He didn't fit in and told God him he didn't want to work for man anymore but for Him. So, he stepped out on faith and God gave him what he asked. His family moved back to Killeen and God blessed him to not have to work anymore, and his family was taken care off. Always be open-minded to change in your life and trust and believe that God will take care of you. Also, be patient, don't rush the process and don't try to do it your way.

## Prayer

*God, we thank You for this day and for who You are in our lives. We ask in the name of Your Son Jesus that You would open our eyes from the blindness and see what You want us to see, and not what we want to see. God, we want to understand Your plan for our life. God we understand that You have already drawn the map and You are the GPS giving us the direction You want us to go. God let us walk in faith and do our natural part so that You can do the supernatural and be providential in our lives. God let us be open-minded to the changes that need to be made in our lives, for we know that it is good and Father give us patience to run this race and journey and we thank You for Your plan and purpose for us in the name of Jesus we pray.*

Amen

### Scripture References:

Psalms 75:8, 25:14, Luke 3:6, 21:19, 1 Corinthians 1:21, Job 40:13, Proverbs 3:32, 9:17, Job 15:8, Matthew 6:6, Romans 5:3-4, 2 Peter 1:6, James 1:3, James 1:4, Colossians 1:11

# CHAPTER 9
# Erasing the Issue By Medicine or Miracle

*You Can Depend on God*

This one thing you can rest your mind on, you can depend on God in any situation. We must develop a dependence on God and not on people because people can and will disappoint you and let you down. God will never let you down, even when you have nothing left or when making hard decisions. Chris had to get out of the military medically because the military felt he was used up. At the end of the day, it was all God, and part of the plan and map for his life.

Even when Chris decided to move from San Antonio back to Killeen, he trusted God during the process. Chris remembers his Bishop having a conversation with him before he transitioned from San Antonio, that if it was meant to be to move back to Killeen or even stay in San Antonio it will line up. Going back to Killeen, everything they asked God for lined up from the house his wife wanted to rent, to the schools for the kids.

Chris had a dependency on God and quickly knew at an early age that he is nothing without him. Before this all came about

Chris and some friends were traveling one night on the way to California to a function for musicians called NAMM. Getting on I-10 in San Antonio he got in an accident that could have taken his life, but God. So, the next morning after the accident Chris took his wife's car to Killeen to a conference his home church, CHOP had it every year called Leaders that Lead. He felt God told him to and there was a word there for him. The word was, when God tells you to do something you do it. The Lord told Chris to come on back to Killeen and it was crystal clear what God was speaking, his assignment in San Antonio was done and it was time for what my fellow veterans would say, return to home base for new training and orders.

After much praying, fasting, and reading the word of God for three months prior to the move, after stepping away from his job at VA, God spoke and confirmations followed, and everything lined up for Chris and his family. So, you see you can depend on God to answer you and give you directions. Even when you are going through your storms from your diagnosis depend on God for strength to see you through, rejoice while in the storm and wait for the manifestation of healing. Lean and depend on God, and how we do this is through prayer, studying the Word, faith, trusting God even when you can't trace Him and through supplication.

### Don't Look Back, Look Forward and Step Out on Faith

Don't look back but step out on faith, depend and trust God. Look forward like Chris did and see the hand of God at work in your life. If we look back, you can miss God and your blessing. Remember the story of Peter walking on water. He looked down for a moment and he started to sink. The lesson is don't fear or doubt, and don't take your eyes off of Jesus. Keep your heart stayed on Him. We can't go back to Egypt for we must move forward to Canaan, our promised land. When we step out on faith that is when God moves.

Chris and his wife were believing God for a home but were so stuck on the price when God told him not to worry about it. Chris was disobedient trying to stay in a certain range, he couldn't close three times on the wrong house and this caused frustration and anger. Chris knew he messed up trying to do it his way instead of God's way, so he got back on track. He and his wife prayed, and God brought them out to a town called Pflugerville, a little town before Austin, Texas. They stepped out on faith and started building the home not worrying about the price but letting God be God.

Over the course of those ten months it took to build the home, Chris would drive out once a month and pray over the land and pour anointing oil over it. He also brought one of his Elders out to pray with him and his wife. One day, Chris was at home praying and he called his wife during her lunch and said, "Sweetie, I am going to step out on faith and start packing the house up."

Chris' wife said, "We haven't even heard from the underwriter yet, but she said, ok I am in agreement with you."

So Chris packed and later that same night they went to Bible study at church. During the sermon, Chris's wife for some reason checked her phone, something she doesn't do often during church services. She went to her email and the manager had emailed them. The email said, I want to be the first one to tell you that you guys were approved for your home. They were blown away by it and just grateful, in awe of what God had done.

Because, Chris stepped out on faith earlier that day and packed, God showed up later that night. God saw his faith because Chris stepped out. This is the secret to faith. We say, I have faith in God, but faith without works is dead. We think faith is saying it and waiting on God, when actually God is waiting on us to step out. He needs to see you step out naturally and then He moves supernaturally. Faith is saying, doing, giving something. Next time you want something or are believing God for healing in your diagnosis, step out on faith show God you depend on, trust, and believe in Him for what He will do for you. My question is, What Are You Waiting For? Step out and watch God blow your mind like He did for Chris and his family.

## Prayer

*We thank You for the dependency on You and being able to trust You. Thank You for allowing us to step out on faith and show You that we are not afraid to trust You in our situation. We believe You Father and every word that You have spoken over us. Help us to see You in a different perspective God You are real, and we know that You can do the impossible in our diagnosis and in our everyday lives. We thank You and love You for it's in Your Son Jesus' name we pray and ask.*

*Amen*

### Scripture References:
1 Corinthians 7:26, 2 Corinthians 3:17, Ephesians 2:8,
Hebrews 11:1-6, John 3:16, Matthew 21:21, 17:20, Galatians
James 2:17, Romans 1:17, Mark 11:22
Peter walking on water, Matthew 14: 22-36

## CHAPTER 10

# The Victory – Overcoming the Diagnosis

*Living Your Life With No Limit*

We often go through life at times wishing we could change the past or do something over again. We also find ourselves saying, is this it, is this all that I am meant to do. When you say that, you are limiting yourself and limiting God. God wants us to live our lives without limits. Even going through our situations and diagnosis we can still live without limits. We put the limits on God because we choose to limit God. Why would you limit a limitless God, that can heal you, He has the cure for your diagnosis? We look at Chris's life and we see what God has done for him. Why? We see this because Chris chose to take the limits off of God and because of that he was healed of the Migraines, PTSD, MTBI, and all of the other issues that he has gone through.

One of the biggest milestones in his life was getting his relationship with his natural father back on track. Today, Chris

*Overcoming the Diagnosis*

and his dad are doing better, they talk, laugh, and have healed from the past hurts and pain. Chris is also doing better with his mother and his marriage is awesome because of what God has done.

In this book, you have seen God's power and His goodness. The same thing can happen for you if you open up your heart and mind and be open to the change. You have to move yourself out of the way because you are what is stopping your growth and holding up God. God wants to bless you in so many ways and do it big. He wants to give you double for your trouble, but we have to go through some hardships and valleys and different diagnosis to get that blessing.

Your story is for His glory and for others to get out of darkness. You are that light torch for those in darkness, that are looking for a way out and a path to escape. You are that avenue that God wants to use. Don't limit yourself to what God can do in you and through you. You have to push past the hurt and pain to see results so why limit yourself if you know that you can go much farther in life.

Look at a bodybuilder, they don't reach that muscle mass overnight. They have to push past the burn and pain while lifting and going beyond it. That track star had to go beyond the pain to get fast and push even harder in the race to achieve the end result. The boxer had to spend hours and days on hand and train for the fight. So, what do these guys have in common, they all went beyond that so-called limit and pushed and believed that there was more. They didn't stop even when they had reached muscle fatigue, they pushed it to the max. That is what we have to do, push past and see the results, when we go beyond that fatigue with that momentum and push, we can see in the end you have more to go.

You only exceed your limit because of you. Don't put the limits and boundaries on your diagnosis but push and go beyond and change your diagnosis. Your diagnosis is what the doctor says it is but what does God say? You can and will overcome your diagnosis like Chris did if you believe and not limit God, believe that all things are possible to those who believe in the impossible, and that my friend, is victory in your diagnosis.

## Smile And Know That You are a Winner

Throughout your diagnosis and journey, you have your days when depression and sadness come and go, but rejoice and smile while you go through. Even if you're going through pain and it hurts, smile and thank God for the pain and the healing. Pain is only temporary it doesn't last forever. You are a winner, a champion, because at the end of your diagnosis the end result is always going to be victory.

Chris had his days with doctors, psychologists and friends and family but he prayed, smiled, and never gave up because he knew the end result of it. He kept focus and didn't let his mind be negative, he allowed his faith to change his diagnosis. Faith changes facts and that is powerful. Chris traced, faced, and erased his diagnosis with God and that is what we all must do to win. We have the strategy and gameplan for our situation, and we need to execute it. Even if it means seeing doctors, go, if it's a change in our lifestyle so be it, if its chemotherapy for that cancer then go through and don't complain. If its mental health issues, then go get help see the psycologist. Do your part and God will do His. He is not a man that He will lie or go back on His promise to heal you and see you through.

*Overcoming the Diagnosis*

We are winners, and this is your winning season, you are the champion, the victor. Why look sad or get mad at the world, why blame people for your diagnosis. Chris could have blamed the military, but he didn't. Nothing happens to us that God has not allowed to happen. Everything is for a reason, there are no surprises to God. He is smiling at you and His angels are pushing you even when you want to throw in the towel. Have patience and run the race, finish and win. No one loses with God because His Son Jesus already won our battle and changed our diagnosis when He gave His life for us so our diagnosis for the doctor was always wrong because God said it was not what man would call it and that my friend is the revelation of a difference. Smile because you have no excuse to complain. You have won!

## Prayer

*Father, we thank You for this day and we ask that You impact our hearts and minds to not limit You and what You can do because You are a limitless God. Help us take the limits off of You and not to give up on You. Abba let our faith change our facts and not our flesh, destroy us, let us go through the diagnosis and smile and laugh and claim victory over every area of our life. Let us be confident and be bold with our faith and speak what You speak and do what You have asked of us. God give us faith to believe and grace to run this race. We thank You for allowing Your Son, Jesus to change our diagnosis so that we could have victory over the diagnosis, Today we are healed and doing better in this season and we are victorious in every area of our life. Bless us in the name of Jesus we ask all, and we smile and rejoice and give You all the praise.*

*Amen*

**Scripture References:**
Proverbs 6:23, 4:18, Jeremiah 32:19, Job 17:12, 1 Timothy 6:16, Exodus 7:20-21, 8: 23-24, 9:22-23, Luke 8:52-55, 10:17-19

# CHAPTER 11

# The New Journey

*Go and Pull Others Out of the Darkness Into the Light*

Throughout this book we have taken a journey through the life of Christ and a few other people and have seen how they have all overcome the diagnosis of life. We have seen the power of God in action and their forward action in trusting Him there are no limits to what He can do. This is the secret to everything that you have gone through, it is not for you, but it is for others. Yes, it was never about you or your situation, but it is for that man or woman who will go through what you have experienced and because you have gone through the valley and come out in victory you can help them. Your testimony can save someone from committing suicide or help give them hope because you have gone through and came out.

There are people who are in darkness like Chris was. You hear so many stories about veterans and people committing suicide, what if you could have said something to them that could have changed their mindset and help save them? Now that you have overcome the diagnosis you are responsible because God has brought you through and showed you how, so now it is your turn to go get someone else who may not know how to get out or overcome their situation. It is amazing because God will bring people to you and it will be like a reflection of yourself. You will encounter people throughout your life who have been diagnosed with your same issues if not similar. You will become attractive and people will be drawn to you because of your light and they will come out of darkness into that light. It can be anywhere, on the job, church, store, park, mall, family reunion, anywhere you must always be ready. God will give you what to speak, sometimes you don't have to say anything at all.

The purpose of this book is to show you that your situation is smaller than God and that you can overcome any situation and diagnosis that life or the doctor will give you. I have seen God move in my life and others. I have watched my Music Director from church be healed of kidney issues and today he is a living, walking, testimony. Him and his wife have overcome many diagnoses. God is real and still in the business of healing and performing miracles. I urge you to share this book with others and plant a seed in someone's life. Remember it was never about you but about God and doing His will and helping others to overcome their diagnosis. Life presents its challenges, but nothing is too hard for God. Thank you for reading this book, you can, and will overcome your diagnosis speak and believe it, and watch God manifest it.

## *Don't Put A Label On Your Diagnosis*

One Last thing let us practice the art of confession there is life and death in what you say. Don't put a label on your situation or diagnosis, reverse it. When you put a label on stuff you are giving it life. Don't say you have PTSD or Cancer just because the doctor says it. We often blame the way we act, or our excuse is that diagnosis. You're putting a label on it and speaking it into existence giving it life, instead speak that you are healed and have faith and are walking it out because God has got you.

My Bishop has taught me that your confession is your possession. We confess with our mouths and possess it and then God will manifest it. God can and will remove that label out of your life if you give it to Him and stay in the positive lane and not the negative. Yes, we may have been diagnosed and labeled by people or the doctor, it doesn't mean we have to accept it because at the end of the day that label or diagnosis does not have us. Our mouth is a powerful weapon along with our mind, speak death to the diagnosis and speak life and healing unto yourself.

Don't speak life to the negative, but speak life and live it and believe it until God brings it to life. Remember that labels are temporary, they can be changed and removed, they are never permanent. Keep your focus on your purpose and stay in the positive lane. Have joy and pleasure in life with God.

## *Prayer*

*God, I thank You for my life and allowing me to see me the way You see me and overcoming the diagnosis. God make me attractive so that people who need help can be drawn to me and can be brought out of their darkness. Father, train my mouth on what to speak, let me never put a label on my issues. Let me speak life and give the diagnosis an expiration date by declaring your word over my diagnosis. In the name of Jesus, I confess and possess and wait until You manifest the total healing and deliverance for my diagnosis. I thank You and praise You in advance for what You will and have done. We love You Jesus and we worship You and believe You and walk in faith. We count it all done in the name of Jesus I pray.*

*Amen*

**Scripture References:**
Psalms 16:11, 52:2, 35:28, Isaiah 53:5, 9:2, Mark 5:34,
John 5:8, 1:5, Ephesians 2:8, Hebrews 11:1-3,
Philippians 4:6 & 13, 2 Corinthians 12:9-10, James 5:16,
Matthew 6:6, Romans 10:10, Job 15:5, 27:4, 33:28,
Proverbs 18:21, 1 Peter 2:9, Luke 1:79

# About the Author

Channing Ewell is a retired Veteran, Purple Heart recipient, man of God, man of Faith, musician, and a living testimony. He is on a mission to help others overcome their fears and diagnosis of their lives.

www.ingramcontent.com/pod-product-compliance
Lightning Source LLC
Chambersburg PA
CBHW050335120526
44592CB00014B/2191